HEALTHY KIDS
TAKING CARE OF
Your Body

Sylvia Goulding

Rourke

Publishing LLC
Vero Beach, Florida 32964

PHOTOGRAPHIC CREDITS
Cover: **The Brown Reference Group plc:** Edward Allwright;
Corbis: (main image) Paul Barton
Title page: **The Brown Reference Group plc:** Edward Allwright
BananaStock: 9, 13, 25, 29; **The Brown Reference Group plc:**
Edward Allwright 1, 4, 5, 6, 7, 8, 9, 10, 12, 15, 16. 17, 18, 20, 24, 28;
Hemera Photo Objects: 9, 10, 11,13, 15, 19, 21, 22, 26, 27;
RubberBall: 3; Simon Farnhell: 5, 6, 7, 11, 25.

FOR ROURKE PUBLISHING LLC
Editor: **Frank Sloan**
Production: **Craig Lopetz**

FOR THE BROWN REFERENCE GROUP PLC
Art Editor: **Norma Martin**
Picture Researcher: **Helen Simm**
Managing Editor: **Bridget Giles**
Design Manager: **Lynne Ross**
Children's Publisher: **Anne O'Daly**
Editorial Director: **Lindsey Lowe**

With thanks to models
**India Celeste Aloysius, Daniel and Lydia Charles,
Zac Evans, Isabella Farnhell, Georgia Gallant,
Lydia O'Neill, Sam Thomson, Connor Thorpe,
and Callum and Joshua Tolley**

Important note: Healthy Kids *encourages
readers to actively pursue good health
for life. All information in* Healthy Kids *is for
educational purposes only. For specific and
personal medical advice, diagnoses, and
treatment, and exercise and diet advice,
consult your physician or school nurse.*

LIBRARY OF CONGRESS CATALOGING-IN-PUBLICATION DATA
Goulding, Sylvia.
  Taking care of your body / Sylvia Goulding.
    p. cm. – (Healthy kids)
  Includes bibliographical references and index.
  ISBN 1-59515-202-4 (hardcover)
  1. Hygiene–Juvenile literature. I. Title. II. Series: Goulding,
Sylvia.
Healthy kids.
  RA780.G68 2004
  613'.0432–dc22

                                        2004012162

Consultant: **Ramona Slick, R.N.,
National Association of School Nurses (NASN)**
*A registered school nurse, Ramona looks
after more than 600 students, from
kindergarten to twelfth grade. Her students
include many with special needs.*

Some words are shown in bold, **like this**. You can find out
what they mean by looking in the glossary on page 30.

Contents

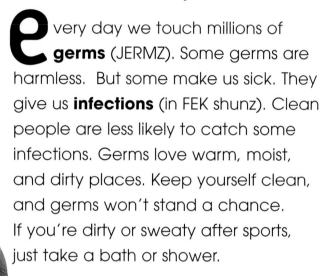

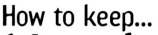
How to keep...
Your body clean

every day we touch millions of **germs** (JERMZ). Some germs are harmless. But some make us sick. They give us **infections** (in FEK shunz). Clean people are less likely to catch some infections. Germs love warm, moist, and dirty places. Keep yourself clean, and germs won't stand a chance. If you're dirty or sweaty after sports, just take a bath or shower.

◀ *Wash your hands with a bar of soap and warm water. The soap takes off most of the dirt. It also makes your hands smell nice.*

Or try this...

- Wash your hands after...
- going to the toilet
- gardening or touching dirt in the yard
- sneezing or coughing

Just amazing!

- No washcloths needed...
- It's easy for a giraffe to clean its ears. Its tongue is 20 inches (50 centimeters) long so it can reach hidden places.

Clean hair and scalp

▶ *Use a comb to remove lice from your hair.*

Healthy hair

Your **scalp** (SKALP) makes oils that protect your hair. When you shampoo, you wash out the dirt. Don't wash your hair too often, however, or you'll wash out the oils that keep it healthy.

Shiny hair

What you eat affects your hair. If your hair looks lifeless, check your dinner. For healthy hair, eat wholegrain food, eggs, oily fish like herring and salmon, carrots, and green vegetables.

Fighting head lice

Head lice pass from person to person. They're irritating but not dangerous. To get rid of them, put on lots and lots of hair conditioner. Then comb the lice out. Repeat until all the lice are gone. Use a pharmacist's product if nothing else works.

hair grows faster in summer

you have 100,000 hairs

each year hair grows 5 inches (12 cm)

▶ *Shampooing and some hair gels can make Afro hair dry. Try petroleum gel to style and protect.*

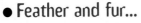

● **Feather and fur...**
- ● Clean out pet cages or huts regularly.
- ● Don't let cats or dogs lick your face.
- ● Wash your hands after touching pets.

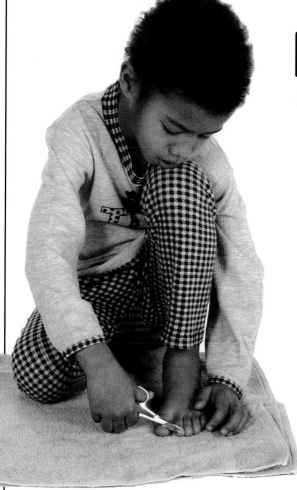

In good hands
Caring for your hands and feet

feet sweat in gym shoes and get smelly. In locker rooms and swimming pools you may catch infections. **Athlete's foot** (ATH leetz FOOT) makes the skin between your toes itchy. Always wash and dry your feet well. Care for your hands, too. Keep them warm and wash them (read about it on page 4).

◀ *Keep your toenails short so you don't hurt your other toes. Cut them straight across the top.*

wash sweaty feet

Just amazing!

● **Amazing feet...**
● Horses walk on tiptoe, called a hoof.
● We walk around 8,000 steps each day.
● A quarter of our bones are in the feet.

Nicer nails...

wear shoes that fit well

▲ *Wear gloves to keep your hands warm in cold weather.*

In Finland Santa brings bad children a bag of toenail clippings.

Nails grow fastest in summer.

Cutting your nails
Shape your fingernails into a gentle curve. Use special nail scissors and a fine nail file.

Chewing nails
Some kids bite their nails because they are nervous. Talking about your worries is better.

Broken and split nails
If your nails break or split, soak them in water. Then rub in a lanolin cream. Eat more cheese and drink more milk. These foods contain **calcium** (KAL see um), which makes your nails strong.

Just amazing!

● **The longest thumbnails...**
A man in India grew the nails of his left hand to a record length. One thumbnail measured 56 inches (142 cm)!

● **Amazing fingernails...**
A doctor can tell from your nails if you are ill. For example, broken nails and white spots mean that you're not eating well.

dry between the toes

◄ Wind, weather, and heating dry your skin. Use skin cream.

In touch with...
Your skin

Your skin is a smart "wrap" around your body. It keeps water and dirt out. It also keeps everything inside your body. Skin sweats to keep you cool you when it's hot. It makes goosebumps to keep you warm. If you scrape your knee, it makes a **scab** (SKAB) and heals over. Your skin is made up of **cells** (SELLZ). Every day, we shed dead cells and grow new ones.

Or try this...

● Natural skin care...
● Before showering, brush your skin with a soft brush. Start at your feet and work up. This brushes away dead skin cells.

Safety first!

● Remember...
● The sun is strong even when it's hazy.
● Winter sun can burn you, too.
● Sun is extra strong near water or snow.

Sun and skin

Is the sun good for me?
Sun makes us healthy and happy. But the sun's rays are strong and can be dangerous. Make sure your skin never burns.

How long can I be in the sun?
Start with just a few minutes on the first day. Slowly increase your time in the sun. Stay out of the midday sun, from noon to 3:00 p.m.

What should I wear?
In the sun, wear a large, light sunhat. A straw hat is good. Wear loose-fitting cotton or linen clothes.

◄ *Pale, freckled skin—stay in the sun for short times only. Use a cream with factor 30–40.*

◄ *Light brown skin—you can stay in the sun a little longer, but you still need to use a factor 15–20.*

◄ *Darker skin—the darker your skin, the longer it takes to burn. Factor 10 should be strong enough. But be careful.*

▶ *Suncream is fun and looks cool!*

- **If you do get sunburned...**
- Apply calamine lotion to the burn.
- Cover up with loose clothing.
- If the burn is severe, see a physician.

Looking after...
Your eyes

Your eyes are like windows to the world. They make you see people and things around you. But sometimes things go wrong. What you see is blurry, or not in **focus** (FO kus). Regularly visit an **optometrist** (op TOM uh trust) for an eye check. In most cases a pair of glasses will help you see better.

◄ *Reading does not make you nearsighted. But always make sure you read in good light.*

Don't try this...

- What makes your eyes red and tired...
- hours staring at the television or the computer screen
- lots of smoke or dust in the air

Safety first!

- Bright sunshine...
- ...can be harmful to your eyes. Wear cool shades to protect them, especially at the seaside or in the snow.

Problem eyes

If you are nearsighted...
You can see things clearly close up. Everything that's far away is blurred. Glasses can help you see better.

If you are farsighted...
You can see faraway things, but what's in front of you is all fuzzy. Glasses can help you see better.

If you are color blind...
Few color-blind people see the world in black and white. But they can't make out one or more colors—either red, blue, or green. In this circle some can't see a number.

If you have a squint...
One eye looks a different direction from the other.

Carrots and other orange foods are great for your eyes. They help you see at night. They stop night blindness.

● **Eat orange-colored fruits and vegetables...**
● Apricots, mangoes, melons, oranges, and carrots are all rich in vitamin A. It helps you see well, especially in the dark.

▶ *Glasses are cool. They help you see better.*

Taking care of...
Your ears

the ears have a double task: they help you hear and they give you balance. They give you pleasure when you listen to music. And they help you back on your feet when you're dizzy after a funfair ride. But watch out: loud noise is bad news. Your ears can get damaged so badly you won't be able to hear well when you get older.

▶ *Enjoy your favorite singer or band. But keep the volume nice and low so you don't stress out your ears—or your parents!*

Safety first!

● **To stop ears popping on a plane...**
...suck on a candy and swallow. Or yawn. Or hold your nose, take a mouthful of air, and blow it out through your nose.

● **There's something in my ear...**
Hold the ear up and pour in lukewarm water. What's in your ear floats out with the water. If it doesn't, see the doctor.

Ear problems

Earache

If your ear is swollen, red, or painful, tell your physician. You might have an infection. The physician will prescribe some medicine. He or she will tell you what you should do and what you shouldn't do to make your ear get better.

Ear wax

Everyone has small amounts of ear wax. It builds up inside your ear and then drops out. If yours doesn't, put a couple of drops of olive oil in your ear every night to soften the wax. If you still have problems, go to see the nurse.

▶ *Don't put anything inside your ears, not even cotton swabs.*

1 elephants use their ears as fans

2 the smallest bone is in the ear

3 an earache can make you feel dizzy

Just amazing!

● **Name that tune...**

Babies can hear music even before they are born. And they can tell when they hear the same tune again!

Looking after...
Your mouth

When you first meet people, give them a warm smile, with two rows of healthy, gleaming white teeth. Brush your teeth thoroughly, from the **gums** (GUMZ) to the tip. If you don't brush, germs collect on and around your teeth and near your gums. This is called **plaque** (PLAK). It rots your teeth. If it gets really bad, your teeth will drop out.

◄ *Brush your teeth twice a day and after meals. Thoroughly clean the front and back of each tooth. Brush the tops of your teeth, too.*

Or try this...

● **Care for your lips...**
Your lips may crack in cold weather and in the sun. Use a sunblock and keep lips moist with a salve or cream.

Safety first!

● **Stop plaque...**
● Brush twice a day and after meals.
● Floss thoroughly between your teeth.
● Visit your dentist at least twice a year.

Seeing the dentist

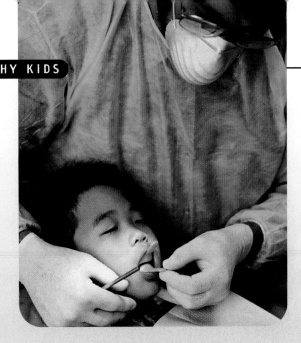

Toothache

Do your teeth feel painful when you eat or drink something hot, cold, or sweet? It can be a sign of **tooth decay** (TOOTH dih KAY). The dentist might give you a filling.

Gum disease

If you don't brush well, your gums can get sore and infected. They will bleed when you brush. The dentist will show you how to brush properly.

▼ Candy, cakes, cookies, and cola drinks are full of sugar, which rots your teeth. Brush thoroughly after eating them. Or, don't eat them at all.

Crooked teeth

If your teeth are not in perfect shape, the **orthodontist** (OR thuh DONT ist) may give you dental braces to wear. They improve your teeth.

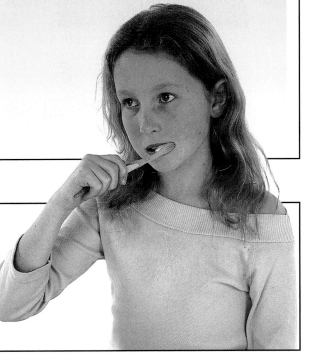

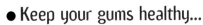

- **Keep your gums healthy...**
- Gently brush your gums and your teeth.
- Use a new brush every three months.
- Don't eat any candy.

Feeding...
Your body

eating healthy food is cool. It stops you getting ill. It gives you strong bones and makes you grow. Eating the right food even makes you smart and look good. You can think better if you eat a good breakfast. Your hair grows shiny, and your fingernails don't break. Don't snack on junk food—it makes you tired, unfit, and overweight.

◀ *Healthy meal— colorful vegetables and salad, grilled chicken, and orange and mango juice.*

▶ *Unhealthy meal— burger and heaps of fries, soft white rolls, tomato sauce, mayo, and cola drink.*

Do eat this...

- **Try to eat plenty of these foods...**
- fruits and vegetables: Chew on fresh or dried fruits instead of snack bars. Pile salad and vegetables high on your plate.
- wholegrain food and **legumes** (leh GOOMZ)—brown grains, lentils, peas
- vegetable oils—Brazil nuts, olives
- Drink fresh fruit juice and water.

Food facts

What you need...

Starchy food
Eat plenty of wholegrain bread, rice, and pasta, and potatoes.

Fruits and vegetables
Eat at least five portions a day. Choose foods of different colors.

Proteins
Eat two servings a day of meat, fish, milk, cheese, or legumes like peas and lentils.

eat lots of fruit and vegetables **1**

Fats
Eat as little fatty food as you can. Avoid animal fats. Choose healthy fats, in nuts, olives, and oily fish.

eat wholegrain foods **2**

Don't eat this...

- **Try not to eat any or only few...**
- fatty and fried food—burgers, fries, hot dogs, chicken nuggets, fish sticks
- snack foods—chips, crackers

- sugary food—cakes, cookies, granola bars
- sauces—mayo, ketchup
- sugary drinks—colas, sodas, flavored waters, fruit drinks without real fruit

avoid fats and sugars

Get active for life

To stay healthy you need to get active. If you don't like school sports, there are lots of other things you can do. Strong muscles can protect you from injury and broken bones. Super-speed and staying power keep your lungs and heart fit. Being active helps you think better. It also makes you look fit. Here are lots of cool ideas for what to do.

18

Exercising your body

Fitness facts

Strong muscles
Lie on your back and air-bicycle. Pull a friend on a toboggan. Row across a lake or hop on one leg.

Sensational super-speeds
Race your pals around the yard, across the swimming pool, on a skateboard, a bike, or up a hill. Or race against yourself.

Stunning staying power
If you get out of breath easily, you need to improve your fitness. Try swimming, running, or dancing. Skip the elevator—walk up the stairs.

Fabulously flexible
Stay flexible. Stretch up on tiptoes. Kick box the air. Bend your body forward, backward, and sideways. Practice keeping up a hula hoop.

◄ *When you're cycling or skating wear a helmet and knee pads. Always stay with an adult at lakes and swimming pools.*

1 be active every day

2 vary your activities

3 do at least 20 minutes each day

Or try this...

- Exercising your mind...
- Set up a crossword tournament.
- Play a memory game—remember as many of the 50 states as you can.

- Get creative—try dancing, singing, writing stories, or painting.
- Learn to play thinking games like chess.
- Play theater and take on different roles.

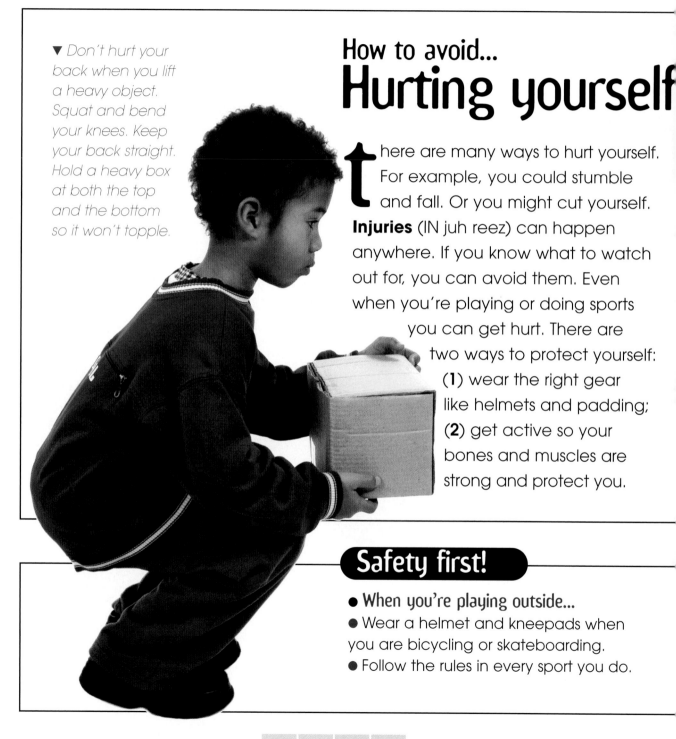

▼ Don't hurt your back when you lift a heavy object. Squat and bend your knees. Keep your back straight. Hold a heavy box at both the top and the bottom so it won't topple.

How to avoid...
Hurting yourself

there are many ways to hurt yourself. For example, you could stumble and fall. Or you might cut yourself. **Injuries** (IN juh reez) can happen anywhere. If you know what to watch out for, you can avoid them. Even when you're playing or doing sports you can get hurt. There are two ways to protect yourself: **(1)** wear the right gear like helmets and padding; **(2)** get active so your bones and muscles are strong and protect you.

Safety first!

● When you're playing outside...
● Wear a helmet and kneepads when you are bicycling or skateboarding.
● Follow the rules in every sport you do.

Every year more than 3.5 million children under 15 years old are treated for sports injuries.

Be careful...

In the house

Be careful around the stove so you don't knock any pots or pans over. Put your toys away so you don't trip over them. Don't kick balls around the house. You could break something and hurt yourself.

In the yard

Many plants are poisonous. Don't eat them unless an adult has told you it's safe. Be especially careful near water. Don't play in sheds or with garden tools. They cause many injuries.

▼ *If you hurt yourself, get help. A clean wound heals faster.*

• Be very careful in traffic. Don't run into the road after balls or pets.
• If you're playing on ice or water, make sure a responsible adult is watching you.

▶ *Never, ever play with chemicals or electrical equipment.*

Staying away from...
Dangers

Life is fun—most of the time. But you need to stay away from some bad things. Don't drink alcohol or smoke. They can make you very ill. Don't let your friends push you into drinking or smoking. Be tough and say "no." Don't let other people upset you. If they want to do something to you that you don't like, walk away. Get help. And: never take any **drugs** (DRUGZ)!

◀ *Stay away from the medicine cabinet. Never take any medicines unless your parents or a physician have told you to.*

Don't ever try this...

● **Dangerous people...**

● You body is yours alone. No one should touch you in a way you don't like. If someone does, tell a teacher or parent.

● Don't ever walk off or drive away with anyone you don't know.

● Don't ever agree to meet up with anyone you meet on the Internet.

Don't smoke

Smoking can kill...

Smoking stinks! It gives you bad breath. It stains your teeth. It costs lots of money. And it can kill you. Cigarettes have two bad ingredients: **nicotine** (NIK uh teen) and **tar** (TAR). Nicotine makes you **addicted** (uh DIKT ud). Tar gives you clogged arteries, heart disease, stroke, and lung cancer.

Don't drink alcohol

Alcohol can kill...

Even if your pals sometimes try a glass of beer, just say "no." Alcohol gives you bad breath and a beer belly. It makes you act stupid or fall over. If you drink too much, you feel ill. Alcohol can make you addicted. It can make you worried and unhappy. It can give you liver disease, stroke, heart disease, and cancer.

Safety first!

- **What to do in an emergency...**
- Call 911 for police, fire, or ambulance.
- Tell the operator exactly what's wrong.
- Tell him or her where you are.
- Stay there so the police, firefighters, or ambulance can find you.
- Try to keep calm.
- Help if you can.

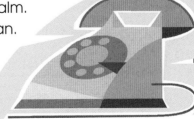

Body and mind at ease

Staying healthy and fit is a good start for a healthy, happy mind. If you feel too much **stress** (STRESS), you get moody or angry. You snap at friends, you cry a lot, and you have bad dreams. Stress can even make you ill. Learn to unwind. There are many ways to do this. If you have a serious problem, seek help.

◄ *Join a class and learn **yoga** (YO guh) for kids. It unwinds body and mind.*

get a good night's sleep

Or try this...

- **You can relax by...**
- running up a few flights of stairs
- having a warm bubble bath
- stroking your cat or dog

- tidying up your bedroom
- doing some gardening
- going for a walk in the countryside
- visiting friends and chatting with them

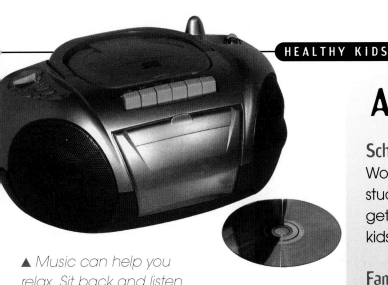

▲ *Music can help you relax. Sit back and listen to your favorite tunes. Or sing along as loud as you can!*

eat healthy food

▶ *Drawing is a fast way out of a bad mood. Or read a funny book that you enjoy.*

A stressful life...

School problems
Worried about tests? Plan your studies to help you pass. Don't get along with a teacher or other kids? See the guidance counselor.

Family problems
Stressed because your parents argue or are getting divorced? Ask a family counselor for help.

Safety first!

- **Help with big problems...**
- Speak to the guidance counselor if you are being bullied by other children.
- See a physician if you're very unhappy.

- If you're being **abused** (ab YOOZD) call: Child Abuse Hotline 1-800-422-4453.
- If you've run away from home call: Runaway Hotline 1-800-621-4000.

do some exercises

Health people...
Caring for you

hundreds of people work all day every day to make sure that you will not get ill. And if you do feel unwell, they are there to help. They can check all parts of your body, inside and out. And they'll give you the best medicine and treatment to make you feel better again quickly.

◀ *If you're sick you may have to stay in a hospital. Nurses will take your temperature if you have a fever. Physicians will check you every day.*

Did you know?

● **Other health workers...**
Many more people work in health. Some are **specialists** (SPESH uh lists). They know all about one part of health.

● There are heart specialists, blood specialists, and back specialists. Some doctors are specialists for children's or women's diseases.

Who's who?

Physicians

They help you get better when you are ill. And they give you **vaccines** (vak SEENZ) to stop you catching certain diseases.

School nurses

They watch your health at school. They measure and weigh you.

Optometrists

They treat you for eye problems and order glasses.

Dentists

They check and polish your teeth.

▶ *A dentist can explain to you what he will do. Electric brushes don't hurt!*

More than 800,000 physicians work in family practices and hospitals all over the country.

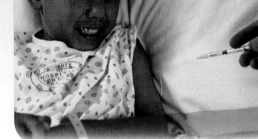

◀ *Injections might be painful. But they can stop you getting ill or help you get better again quickly.*

Just amazing!

● The physician may examine you to find what's wrong. He may check your blood or urine for diseases. Or he may take an **X ray** (EKS RAY) of the inside of your body.

● **Live a long and healthy life...**

● A French woman, Jeanne Calment, was one of the oldest women ever. She died in 1997, when she was 122 years old!

Take care of your body for..
A happy life

looking after your body is not hard. Just follow the ideas in this book: eat well, sleep well, keep yourself clean, and get lots of exercise. The rewards come straight away. You'll stay healthy. You'll look good and feel good. You'll have bundles of energy to work and play.

◀ *Healthy kids have lots of friends because they enjoy playing together.*

sleep well 2

Safety first!

● **Tell your physician if...**
● You don't feel well most days.
● You suffer from aches and pains and don't know why.

● **Tell the school nurse if...**
● You gain or lose a lot of weight.
● You've hurt yourself at school.
● You have any health questions.

Test yourself

1. Which of these sentences is true?

A You should wash your hands at least once every hour during the day.

B You should wash your hands after you've been to the toilet.

C You should wash your hands after you've stroked a pet.

2. To be fit and healthy you need:

A three hours at the gym every day

B 20 minutes of activity a day

C half an hour of sports a month

3. Which are good foods to eat?

A plenty of fruits and vegetables of different colors

B burgers, fries, hot dogs, sodas

C wholemeal bread, brown rice, pasta, and potatoes

4. If you're all stressed out, you should...

A Pull yourself together and stop moaning all the time.

B Try something relaxing, like yoga or going for a walk.

C Go to a hospital for an operation.

5. Match these jobs to what they look after:

A dentist   a eyes

B optometrist   b vaccinations

C physician   c teeth

ANSWERS: 1B and C, 2B, 3A and C, 4B, 5: Ac, Ba, and Cb.

● **Tell your parents if...**

● You get so worried you can't sleep.

● You've got problems with your friends.

● You're really happy!

◀ *Healthy kids are smart and get good grades at school.*

29

Glossary
What does it mean ?

abused: *Being treated badly or cruelly.*
addicted: *If you cannot stop taking something you are addicted to it.*
athlete's foot: *A disease that makes the skin between the toes cracked and itchy.*
calcium: *Calcium makes healthy teeth and bones. Milk and cheese contain calcium.*
cell: *The smallest building block in our body. Your body contains billions of cells.*
drugs: *Illegal chemicals that addict people.*
focus: *Something is in focus if you can see it clearly.*
germs: *Very tiny living things that can make you ill. Bacteria and viruses are germs.*
gums: *The firm pink flesh around teeth.*
infections: *Diseases caused by germs.*
injury: *Damage or harm.*

legumes: *Beans, lentils, and peas.*
nicotine: *A dangerous chemical in tobacco. It makes you addicted.*
optometrist: *A specialist who checks your eyesight and orders glasses if you need them.*
orthodontist: *A dentist who improves crooked teeth.*
plaque: *A sticky layer of food and bacteria on the surface of teeth.*
scab: *Dried blood that hardens and covers a cut or sore. Scabs help wounds heal.*
scalp: *The skin on top of your head.*
specialists: *People who learn more about one part of health. They become experts.*
stress: *A lot of worry, or great pressure.*
tar: *A dangerous chemical in tobacco. Tar damages lungs, with which you breathe.*
tooth decay: *A disease that rots your teeth.*
vaccines: *Injections to stop you getting ill.*
X ray: *An image that sees through your skin.*
yoga: *Exercises for body and mind. They help you relax all over.*

To find out more...

...check out these books:
● Bagley, Katie. *Brush Well: A Look at Dental Care.* Bridgestone Books, 2002.
● Bagley, Katie. *Keep Clean: A Look at Hygiene.* Bridgestone Books, 2002.
● Buckley, Annie. *Kids Yoga Deck: 50 Poses and Games.* Chronicle Books, 2003.
● Douglas, Ann and Julie Douglas. *Body Talk.* Maple Tree Press, 2002.
● Seuling, Barbara. *From Head to Toe:*

To find out more...

...check out these websites

● www.cdc.gov/tobacco/sgr/sgr4kids/sgrmenu.htm
The Surgeon General's Report for Kids about Smoking.

● www.kidshealth.org
Click on these links for info on smoking, alcohol, and about your teeth:
www.kidshealth.org/kid/watch/house/smoking.html
www.kidshealth.org/kid/grow/drugs_alcohol/alcohol.html
www.kidshealth.org/kid/body/teeth_noSW.html

● www.therolemodelprogram.org/kids_section.shtml
The Role Model Program—Kids Section

● http://smilekids.deltadentalca.org/index.html
Smile Kids—Dental Health

● www.cyh.com/cyh/kids/index.html
Child and Youth Health—Kids Only Section

● www.uhrad.com/kids.htm
X Rays for Kids

The Amazing Human Body and How it Works. Holiday House, 2002.
● Sluke, Sara Jane and Vanessa Torres. *The Complete Idiot's Guide to Dealing with Stress for Teens.* Alpha Books, 2002.

● Sweet, Julia E. *365 Activities for Fitness, Food and Fun for the Whole Family.* McGraw-Hill, 2001.
● Walker, Richard. *DK Guide to the Human Body.* Penguin Books Ltd, 2001.

Index

Which page is it on?